Sci
Vocabulary Readers

Cool Penguins

Jeff Bauer

SCHOLASTIC INC.

NEW YORK • TORONTO • LONDON • AUCKLAND • SYDNEY
MEXICO CITY • NEW DELHI • HONG KONG • BUENOS AIRES

ISBN-13: 978-0-439-87647-6 / ISBN-10: 0-439-87647-8

Photos Credits:
Cover: ©; Stele/Getty Images; title page: © Theo Allofs/Corbis; contents page, from top: © Colin Monteath/Headgehog House/Minden Pictures, © Getty Images, © Kevin Schafer/Corbis, © Roland Seitre/Peter Arnold Inc.; page 4: © Getty Images; page 5, top left: © Corbis; page 5, top right: © Tom Vezo/Peter Arnold Inc.; page 5, bottom left: Tom Vezo/Peter Arnold Inc.; page 5, bottom right: © Doug Cheeseman/Peter Arnold Inc.; page 6: © Colin Monteath/Headgehog House/Minden Pictures; page 7: © Tui de Roy/Minden Pictures; page 8, left: © Kelvin Aitken/Peter Arnold Inc.; page 8, right: © Rinie Van Meurs/Foto Natura/Minden Pictures; page 9, left: © Daniel J. Cox/Natural Exposures; page 9, right: © Kevin Schafer/Corbis; page 11: © Getty Images; page 12: © Getty Images; page 12, inset: © Frans Lanting/ Minden Pictures; page 13, top: © Norbert Wu/Minden Pictures; page 13, bottom: © Getty Images; page 14: © Kevin Schafer/Corbis; page 15: © Tui de Roy/Minden Pictures; page 16, top: © John Conrad/Corbis; page 16, bottom: © Daniel J. Cox/Natural Exposures; page 17: © Frans Lanting/Corbis; page 18: © Norbert Wu/Minden Pictures; page 19 © Roland Seitre/Peter Arnold Inc.; page 20: © Wolfgang Kaehler/Corbis; page 20, inset: © Bill Curtsinger/Getty Images; page 21: © Galen Rowell/Corbis; page 22: © Peter Johnson/Corbis; page 22, inset: © Corbis; page 24: © Getty Images; back cover: Art Wolfe/Getty Images.

Photo research by Dwayne Howard
Design by Holly Grundon
Map by Jim McMahon

12 11 10 9 8 7 6 5 4 7 8 9 10 11 12/0

Printed in the U.S.A.
First printing, January 2007

Contents

Chapter 1

Meet the Penguin

Penguins hop, slip, and slide. Penguins swim, leap, and dive. What kind of animal do you think they are?

All of these are birds.

Penguins are birds! They have feathers and lay eggs. But they cannot fly.

Fast Fact

There are more Adélies (a-**dey**-leez) **than any other kind of penguin.**

This picture shows Adélie penguins. You may have seen them at the zoo. But there are many other types of penguins, too.

Emperor penguins are the largest. Some of them weigh 100 pounds. That is as much as a big dog!

Fast Fact

Why do you think these penguins were given these names?

fairy penguin

rockhopper penguin

Fairy penguins are the smallest. They weigh only as much as a kitten. There are also rockhopper penguins. The bright feathers on top of their head are called a **crest**.

chinstrap penguin

black-footed penguin

Let's not forget about chinstrap penguins and black-footed penguins. There are 17 kinds of penguins in all!

Chapter 2

Survival Skills

The red shows where penguins live in the world.

Penguins can be found in some of the coldest places on the planet. They are one of the few animals that can live in **Antarctica**.

Penguins have thick feathers to keep out the cold. A layer of fat underneath the feathers also helps them to stay warm.

List

Penguin Predators

- leopard seals
- orcas
- sea lions
- sharks

Penguins have dark backs and light bellies. This special coloring lets them blend in on land and sea. It helps penguins hide from **predators** that want to gobble them up.

List

Penguin Food

- fish
- krill
- squid
- octopus
- small sea creatures

Penguins use their flippers and webbed feet to swim super-fast. They use their sharp beaks to grab an underwater lunch.

Chapter 3

On the Move

Penguins have plenty of ways to move on land and in the sea. They can dive. They can swim on top of the water or deep underneath it.

Fast Fact **Penguins can hold their breath underwater for 20 minutes!**

Three penguins leap out of the water after a swim.

And guess what? When penguins are done swimming, they can leap right out of the water onto a snowbank. Wow!

waddle

hop

On land, penguins **waddle** to get around.
They are also great hoppers.

Penguins can even flop on their bellies and slide. Weeee! This is called **tobogganing**.

Chapter 4

Penguin Chicks

Most kinds of penguins make nests out of rocks, sticks, or dirt. Each nest holds one or two eggs.

Fast Fact

Some penguins steal rocks from other penguins to build bigger nests.

Both the male and female take turns keeping the eggs warm. One penguin parent stays home while the other hunts for food.

A newborn penguin chick looks like this.

The eggs are ready to hatch after one or two months. Chicks break through the eggshells with their sharp little beaks. Chip, chip, chip! This is called **pipping**.

Chicks are covered in a soft fuzz called down.

The chicks start singing as soon as they hatch. The parents sing back. This helps the new penguin family learn one another's voices.

A chick finds its mom.

Even in a huge crowd, a parent and chick can find each other by singing. Penguins are very cool birds indeed!

Glossary

Adélie penguin (a-**dey**-lee **pen**-gwin): a type of penguin that lives in Antarctica

Antarctica (ant-**ark**-tic-a): a cold, icy continent that covers the South Pole

crest (**krest**): a tuft of feathers on top of a bird's head

down (**doun**): the soft fluffy feathers of a penguin chick

pipping (**pip**-ing): when a penguin uses its beak to hatch out of an eggshell

predator (**pred**-uh-tur): an animal that hunts another animal for food

tobogganing (tuh-**bog**-uhn-ing): when a penguin slides over ice on its belly

waddle (**wahd**-uhl): to take short steps and sway from side to side

Comprehension Questions

1. Can you name three kinds of penguins?
2. Can you name three penguin parts?
3. Can you name three ways that penguins get around?
4. Can you share three facts about baby penguins and their parents?

Bonus Penguin Facts

- Some penguins live to be 20 years old.
- As many as one million penguins sometimes crowd together in one place.
- Penguins can drink saltwater! They have special glands to remove the salt.